Rotura

Rotura

José Angel Araguz

www.blacklawrence.com

Executive Editor: Diane Goettel
Cover Design: Zoe Norvell
Book Design: Amy Freels
Cover Art: "Trial by Fire, Series 30 #1" by Heather Goodwind

Published 2022 by Black Lawrence Press.
Printed in the United States.

para Manuel, vatako y hermano en palabras

You build the fence we climb the fence
You hammer it up we rock it down
You draw the line we erase the line
You reinforce it we loosen it
You block it we dig under it
You use nightvision we use huaraches
You use bomb-smelling dogs we use chorizo-scented cucarachas
You ask Are you an American citizen? we say Yes way before you

—Juan Felipe Herrera "Mexican Differences Mexican Similarities"

Contents

A Question Before the Election   1

Language Dirge   19
Four Dirges   20
Birthday Dirge   25
In the margins, with blackberries   27

October, Before the Election   31
American Studies   32
Engrossed   34
A Poco   36
Race   37
Conditioning (Run Study)   39
Conditioning (City Study)   42

Certain Rivers   47

Snow in December   55
En la colonia I cannot find   56
Roaches   59
Night Matter   60
Selena: a study of recurrence / worry   61
In the margins, with birds   63

Coconut   64

Disrepair   66

Arguing for the Stars   67

Conditioning (Air Study)   68

On the Times I Don't Remember the Right
                Words for Things   72

Saudade   77

Questions After the Election   91

Notes, Credits, Acknowledgments   96

A Question Before the Election

my mother asks if I've heard of the KKK—

a month later the election will turn in favor of a man

endorsed by them / a month later my wife and I will begin unpacking

how we represent what is not wanted here

(give us not your disabled nor woman,

not brown skin of self and family

and families) / a month later we will grow quiet

swiping at screens to refresh reality,

hoping the next flash of text and pixels will give us reason

to speak above a mumbled, grit-lined whisper,

to move the air beyond the pause

of remembering to breathe—

because she's heard

of a man who brings the worst

out of people / because she wants

to warn me

but is years late

to shield me from history,

from threats and sideways glances,

outright glares, from nights

of glass bottles broken behind me

thrown from cars crammed with frat boys

yelling: *Go back to your country!*

my mother asks if I've heard of the KKK—

a year later I will be thinking of lists in poems,

what it is one inventories,

makes space for,

stops to see in lists / a year later

I would list different things

my mother and I are years late for:

like me asking what it was like for her

when she first came to this country, or her

asking me why I write, why

I teach, why I do anything but

hide and stay quiet

like she asked me to be

as a child

a year later

I will have been walking

looking over my shoulder

for more than thirty years:

the man I am looking over my shoulder

not noticing that I march behind

the youth-I-was who starved himself,

and hoped to disappear, too busy

looking over his shoulder to know he marched behind

the teen-I-was in black T-shirts

who kept checking and correcting his English

and hating his skin, too in his head

and looking over his shoulder to know

he marched behind the child-I-was

alone in garage apartments staring out

the windows at trees and cars,

ducking down when a cop car passed

and closing his eyes

a year later

it will hit me

that these years of looking over my shoulder

are a list inside me that inventory,

make space for,

stop to see

the fear inside me—

my mother asks if I've heard of the KKK and I feel

the worst has found its way

into my palm, the worst

has me clutching it,

hearing it sounded out

in my mother's voice,

and I know then what I hold

in my hands will continue

to grow heavy—

what I hold in my hand trembles when

I cry / my wife cries / friends

tell me they cried—

when I remember

in a hushed hurried voice

as if we were calling to each other

from different parts of a dark wood

wanting to both call out and be found

but also not draw attention

my mother asking me—

¿has oído del KKK?

I feel

failure

desengaño

loss

decepción

breakdown

caída

defeat

quebrado

collapse

rotura

frustration

amargura

grief

—bueno,

pues,

si—

Language Dirge

each tongue is heard in the river's
lap and lag, and each tongue rises,
becomes more than barbed wire glint,
more than mud and dead grass,

more than traffic and a bridge for traffic,
each tongue swells and pools
to become more than ash hands
knocking at doors of ash,

each tongue would be more

than panic, but the river is not
about being heard, but about being
in motion, in this, the river is
about languages, about

words and breath,

and what can be done
with words and breath,
what can be dredged,

what can be crossed and forgotten,

what can run down from polluted
country to polluted country
until everyone is rooted,
until everything is reflected,

until the river pulls away

Four Dirges

I don't know about gods; but I think that the river
Is a strong brown god—sullen, untamed and intractable...

(T.S. Eliot, "The Dry Salvages" from *Four Quartets*)

Rio Grande, Rio Bravo Dirge

Thomas: It's true, you don't know
about gods beaten and worn
like the space left between
paired jigsaw puzzle pieces
where a child has tried
and tried to force
the wrong piece in;
you might've known about
gods who linger, who know
lightning bolts, who know bargains
and carry swords, but I think you
lacked the capacity to notice
their lack of capacity
to harbor and be a hand
to shade our eyes; shaded now,
you don't know and died
not knowing the slosh of gods
and the dark gleam of gods
that reflect clean off badges
hot over paid hearts.
This river god who rears and waits,
in place like a door left ajar,
god that moves and darkens—
this is not a being of your thoughts.

Water Dirge

Tom: Do you not know that,
before boundaries were decided
between men separating Mexico
and the U.S., there was water?
Before the city lights made us
forget the stars, and before the desert
was made a road, and before people crammed
into trucks and were called cargo,
called *nothing back there, officer,*
there was water? Do you think
water is an argument waged
between two gods?
Think, where I believe,
water is blood spilt
between two gods?
Do you think as I do
that I might mean *split*
and not *spilt*?
Do you know much
about the silence,
so much like a river,
when I've been seen as
sullen, untamed, and intractable—

Nueces River Dirge

Tommy: Is your strong brown god
also this chosen river, split from brother
by distance and legislation,
river that empties into Corpus
Christi Bay? No, I know you spoke
of the Ohio, and I know that river, too.
But what would you call
the hard waters of my home city?
What blessings for us who
offer up nothing but faces
can you think of? What looks back
when we hold water in our hands
and wait, a moment of dark mirror—
that we are then made in the image
of what we cannot utter? That we
are lost in clouded lifelines
as we stand outside a door
we've had no hand in making?

Corpus Dirge (December 2016)

T: When the water was contaminated
in Corpus I did not consider gods,
did not know them or think them
able to help my family who
already had bottled water in bulk,
my mother who made sure
her sons didn't drink
from the tap, who attempted
to shower with bottled water
a few times only to have
to give up, her arms giving out
after double shifts of work. When
the water was tainted I took
the time to look up maps, traced
by zip code the neighborhoods cut
off from water, noted that where
they lived, my family would live
without service for some time.
Same for the neighborhoods
we used to live in, from Leopard
to Greenwood, and yet water
had been restored to areas
I never saw until I had started
driving and would detour
through ritzy residentials,
or so they seemed at sixteen.
When it was tainted, I knew water

had given off light
like roads made of glass
before I was born,
knew that water bore
and took in all that fell
long before I'd fallen off
the map I traced over trying
to think and find any thin
reassurance. When the water
was tainted, it remained water
and would remain water,
and all the words wearing down
in meaning are my family
history, are part of my story—
Mr. Eliot, before I was born
you wrote about a strong brown god
but what are gods when there is water
in rivers who have nothing to do
with what isn't already part of them?
If the *river is within us*, then why
did I fear it killing those I cared for?
Why do gods—beyond belief,
knowledge, and thought—scrawl
out of me, awkward, reverent,
and dying?

Birthday Dirge

August 2017

This is a story about a walk on the beach on my birthday.
As I walked and looked over the Pacific, I hated myself.

I hated myself and hated the ocean, the water turning on itself.
I could only think of how the water in Corpus Christi turned over on itself.

As I walked and looked over the Pacific, I hated myself.
The hurricane turned my mother's voice on the phone into water.

I could only think of how the water in Corpus Christi turned over on itself.
She feared that the door to her house would be pulled off its hinges.

The hurricane turned my mother's voice on the phone into water.
The hurricane turned the door-hinges into fingers tight around a cellphone.

She feared that the door to her house would be pulled off its hinges.
I worried her voice would drop into the static that edged our conversations.

The hurricane turned the door-hinges into fingers tight around a cellphone.
The wind on the Oregon coast became the wind I heard behind my
   mother's voice.

I worried her voice would drop into the static that edged our conversations.
Our conversations turned over in my mind for months after.

The wind on the Oregon coast became the wind I heard behind my
   mother's voice.
I hated myself and hated the ocean, the water turning on itself.

Our conversations turned over in my mind for months after. This is a story about a walk on the beach on my birthday.

In the margins, with blackberries

I feel dirty eating them,
plucking them off the fence
along the cemetery
after work. No one
else comes to eat them.
Before I bite down,
I let each berry linger
on my tongue, the styles
prickling, reaching out
from the flesh. Who can help
what the body remembers,
what bristle and burn,
what colors? Not the seasons.
Not the birds that follow. Not
the leaves finding themselves
flickering, then falling.
I walk past graves of
people I have never known
and think of friends I have,
of how I have never walked
past their graves, of who
might be doing so now.
Rubbing my darkened fingers
against my jeans, no one's
around but I hurry anyway.
Why let them dry up, burst?
Let their sweetness linger
on my fingers, let them
ask for my attention
a few more hours.

October, Before the Election

no one claims responsibility
for the shriveled flowers

the willow considers dropping its leaves early

the wind comes through
holding conversation with itself

the dust mistakes itself for news,
rises and writes out a notice

places it all over the city

American Studies

November 22, 2016

My wife tells me of reading the *Dear
America* books as a child, those stories told
via the diaries of young women who lived

during difficult times in American history. In these
stories filled with suffering were the facts behind
the suffering. Her favorite involved the RMS Titanic,

the unsinkable ship that sank. I ask if
trying to imagine what it looked like was
what captivated, and she says no, says only

one book led to another, until she realized
she could never see it nor accept it.

*

After the election, my friend explains he feels
he could manage here, but not his children.
He explains he spoke to their school director,

who comforted by talking about police presence. But
if there's police, he asks, before anything happens,
what will happen when something does? American algebra:

Everything is x until proven y. Dear America,
if x represents what my friend feels thinking
about the police, what language do you imagine

he worries his children speaking publicly, and what
language are we speaking now? Show your work.

*

Another friend writes: Here's a verse I think
about a lot: *And maybe the mirror of*
the world will clear once again. She shares

she's been sick since the election, as I've
been. I imagine our voices trying to commiserate
between coughs. In physics, energy can neither be

created nor destroyed. What American physics happens here
as I read and hear her voice behind
the verse she sent? Are you, dear America,

afraid as I am that our faces will
no longer be there when the mirror clears?

Engrossed

Grabbing a raincoat, I find a moth and ask:
What do you do here in my closet,
what of your light—

to which he says: *At the end of each night,*
my light goes into my soul, what of
yours? The day is then

the weather's blue colors, mirrors and rain,
that almost white where a thick darkness
blurs with a thick light.

Standing there, I see myself almost a man,
almost a moth, pieces of
a remembered face

brought up, overlapping, as if the changing face
were on old film, and that old film
played across moth wings

holding their position. Almost myself
frame by frame and without sound,
imposed on dust

for an audience. Almost my face holding
still, and face turning away. Face
of wing-wilt and wend.

Grabbing a raincoat, I found a moth and asked
myself about light, and myself answered
light; a moth

throbbed at having been found. When
my words had flickered aloud, the moth,
too, flickered,

an unknown face caught flinching, unfolding
face laughing, face
forgetting its name.

A Poco

for Ramon

This piece of paper is work? A poco?
I won't believe that, ni un poco.

It's work for me with this good eye,
one bad eye from broke glass, pero a poco

tu with two don't struggle here?
And with books and school? A poco

you all talk about it, in class, I mean,
about what it means? That's work. A poco,

I'm not here, you don't write about me,
right? My bad eye? I bet you do. A poco,

no? You have nothing else? You have nothing else.
Don't say it looks like a bruise gone white. A poco,

no? But don't say it. Say it's a marble, or
like my granddaughter says: *A poco,*

you can't see out of that fisheye, abuelo?
Can you see me? Nope. Ni un poco.

Race

You cannot see the miles
in the color of
my skin, cannot see
how fast the river runs
and who can run as fast,
cannot hear how quick
prayers are said, nor how
swift to be forgotten—
headlights speed,
speed of flashing
lights, speed
of feeling
disoriented,
no stars enough
to recall the way,
speed of having
to turn back—
cannot know the work
of generations gone,
unknown, is done in what
I do or don't—speed of
looking back,
speed of passing
signs, speed of
names recalled,
speed of stories told
and told to forget—
another heart racing,
set here to hurt, to laugh,

to break, heart set to
this rhythm, difference,
this rhythm running—
speed of the first breath,
this breath, speed of
the last—
in the color of my skin
not a flush or flicker,
no change but who
I keep becoming
with each hurried,
harried step.

Conditioning (Run Study)

I must run: walking won't get me there.

       Miles must take the place of arms; distance,

embrace. I must run, until I become air.

       Conditioning is a whisper on the eyelash

of an eye that doesn't blink

       afraid of missing seconds pass.

Conditioning is the day spent hinting:

       a bee working his wings to slivers,

a life never done with communicating.

       I had to run with my Mexico and Ginsberg

tucked under my whiskers, run, and sow asterisks

       and metaphors where buttons had fallen off of shirts.

I must run, because all I thirst for

are syllables, and when someone says to me

no vales mierda or *Latino? What's that?* I gulp, keep score.

I must run because footprints don't last long in the sand,

and the desert is larger than people can hurt.

There are days when the sun is a moon I can't understand.

Conditioning is words spoken, unaware

they, like cars, live broken, in need

of constant repair.

Conditioning is being told to drink only white milk

so that your skin might change; this from someone

whose skin matches yours, down to the shame.

I must run, or else I'll always be taking off

      my hat in nice neighborhoods, smoothing down my hair,

always trying to look acceptable, but feeling off.

Conditioning (City Study)

Conditioning is you
looking down Seventh Avenue
at 4am:
          the dawn sky
a plum cracked
and pushed into itself.

*

Conditioning is the man
hosing down the sidewalk
before the sporting goods store

opens, the trash and papers turned
rags, the cans and plastic bags
turned squalid gems, rushed

to the curb and falling
in a hurl
of green-black water.

*

Conditioning is the woman
who stands in a puddle
stopping to see if the man

with the hose will stop,
and when he doesn't,
proceeds to walk into the street.

*

Conditioning is thinking the men
asleep under the stairway,

garbage bag for a shared pillow,
have bodies like fallen dolls.

*

Conditioning is the group of men
in uniforms with WINDOW UNIT
on the back,

and you thinking them
truculent as children
ready to hit something.

*

Conditioning is the woman crouching
over a broken stiletto,
and the man with a hand

on her back saying:
It's ok—spit
against his lips

like foam at the farthest reach of a wave
you were just reading about
on the train.

*

Conditioning is the walk to work
where you look up to Hermes
above Grand Central

his hands frozen mid-wave
as if forever casting a spell
over everything that moves.

*

Conditioning is the voice
you still hear asking:
Who the fuck is you?

Certain Rivers

When it hurts we return to the banks of certain rivers
Czesław Miłosz

When a river's crossed,
how many families hold their breath?

Breath-made rivers they cannot keep inside,
one after another, the only thought: Adelante.

Later, with children,
with hours of work wearing down the body,

these breath-made rivers run through
dreams and stories

they tell their children not to voice—
small faces hold still

while questions begin to course
and shadows dam the back of the throat.

*

I have made a myth of our river;
in telling the myth, one river becomes

many rivers, the one my mother crossed
lost in the one I cross now

in ink. You can't step into the same river twice,
but you can try:

the sound will grow, will lap and splash,
sound of displacement,

sound of will, of wanting, in your mind,
sound of steps going nowhere.

*

Water knows how to be lost,
has a need for it, just watch:

the rain is all scramble and clearing
of tracks; watch a napkin

over a puddle, how water goes for broke
to be lost,

clings, rises,
soaks the fabric, pretending part

like it does in clouds that grow, give,
and clear.

*

Shadow is a kind of water
in that it knows one way to be lost:
Just wait, it says, *just wait.*

*

Water knows its way to truth:
you can see what lies at the bottom

of rivers, you can wash away the dirt
to see your hands again. Water is, then, not

the truth but a way to it; shadow then
is not a lie but something also passing over truth.

Down the street at noon, you cannot look around
without seeing others making the same, strained face.

A country also knows its way to truth,
but can choose to pass over it.

In this country of water and shadow,
truth is strained from our faces.

*

My mother turns to water on the phone,
the river of her voice carries the years between us,

years where I have strained to catch
something of our changing faces.

The river of her voice is a kind of truth I know,
I see what lies at the bottom of these years,

I wash away the dirt
and see my hands tremble.

*

Water knows how to be lost,
has a need for it, but it cannot choose:

a river runs to ocean
and is not lost, just ocean;

a river runs dry and is lost,
you think, but later it returns,

and only then do you ask
what is a river, but never answer,

happy to have the river.
People know how to be lost to others,

crossing rivers helps.
People know, but they must choose,

and, even then, they are not lost
to themselves. Mother, you brought me

with you over water,
over a way to truth,

over the distance of your shadow,
and in shadows now we wait

for the other to call.

*

Sometimes she calls in tears,
and like an earthworm when the rain comes
and fills its burrow, a part of me

works itself out to the surface to breathe.
I can hear the water in her words,
flooding sentences of love

and regret cloud what I know
how to say. Whatever actual clouds
in the distance between her and I

rearrange as she continues
to break and give herself over
to the ten or fifteen minutes it takes

to grieve that one cannot grieve,

       no hay tiempo,
       tus hermanos, esta casa
       nunca está limpia
       no ves
       Cuída bien
       esa niña tuya
       Lo siento
       no hablamos suficiente
       deberíamos
       gente muere, ¿sabes?

I know

this voice from other nights,
other cold moments when I've stopped
in my life to listen, drummed

out from the dirt of where I live
and made to gleam like rain
and worms, glass bottle shards,

the hard face of a television
clicked off to leave a house quiet
but for the pleading half-whisper,

half-snore of a woman
with no time to grieve.

Snow in December

As one fell
and then

another
against

the pane
before him,

he began
to see

in the flakes
the drawn

lines of
eyelashes,

the world now
closing

and closing
its eyes.

En la colonia I cannot find

I dream in a house filled with winter,

       a house always between stages. My tía,

in the country where I am a child,

       watches as her dream house develops:

walls of cardboard and wood planks

       make way for cinderblocks; doors

to each room go from bedsheets

       to knobbed, solid doors; the floor

remains dirt long past childhood,

       past when I stayed there, long into

the stories I hear of deals made

       with narcos to keep safe the house

I used to dream in. Her house different

       each year I slept there, memories

now different colors, the bottoms of

       my feet the color of the earth

I walk across feeling winter, each

       small step picking up more of the earth.

My tía paces, wanting more for herself,

       each step as dark as mine. In dreams,

we talk in the same house I try to place

       years later on a map of Matamoros:

not the crowded colonias near the bridges,

       nor the populated, street-lined center

nor the blocked-off Zona Industrial.

       My eye veers further down dark swaths

of map, unmarked and undeveloped,

       one road straight into the open fields

and ranches of makeshift shacks

       and shacks shifting, made into

the country we find ourselves

       dreaming in now. We counsel

each other in Spanish and English,

       say we did not know, no sabiamos,

what the country would be like,

       nor what would happen there.

We walk amidst changing walls,

       our steps marking the path,

and the path marking our soles,

       the earth molding to where

I relive nights of winter,

       of not knowing

this is the nature of longing,

       of faith, of not being satisfied.

Roaches

Copper-flecked,
I reached for one as a child
to see what luck I had.

Night Matter

In a house without electricity, what matters
is having clean paper, and enough light for words.

Crouched at the window, by the streetlamp's light, I write.
When the light clicks off, ask my hand if it matters.

Even when I can't tell what word lays at my fingers,
I know the force and heat is my matter.

My eyes make out the paper as a glow
registered by some animal sense that makes it matter.

The night sky fills with bits of shell and bone,
or so I write in ink, in night-matter.

Since men learned print, no night is wholly black.
since I learned night, my print is holy matter.

Frost spoke of being *acquainted with the night*;
having words with it, *neither wrong nor right,* is another matter.

You who read and move on to other matters,
the night knows who between us must do the dying.

Selena: a study of recurrence / worry

Somebody died and it's okay to be Mexican.

      No, really, this is good. I was worried

nobody would understand what it means to come

      from a city named after the recurring body

of a martyr. No, really, this is good.

      I worried a whole generation of young women

from a city named for wounds and resurrection

      would suffer themselves to be stilled and lost. Now

I worry a whole generation of friends close

      their fists around empty beer cans and walk

out the door to become lost, distilled memories.

      You would think no one would sing here

again. That with beer cans in their fists

      mothers would tell stories about a ghost

appearing should you sing here in this city,

should you ever go onstage, a whole generation

of mothers telling stories where not a ghost

but a microphone vanishes directly below a spotlight

that burns anyone who walks onstage, different moon

in a different sky where it is always night.

See, a whole city vanishes below the spotlight

of my erratic memory. Corpus Christi, my imagination

paints you as an indifferent sky where night

after night we tell stories about who we were.

You are more than my erratic memory and imagination,

more than the name of a wounded returned body.

When at night I tell stories about Selena,

I know that it is more complicated than

the name on a statue, more complicated than

somebody died, and it's okay to be Mexican.

I know life is more complicated than

anyone can understand or hope to become.

In the margins, with birds

Waiting for the bus is a purgatory in itself,
wind biting at my skin and wounding cold.

February and I cannot believe the sky can hold
so many birds and not choke out feathers for rain.

Hemingway had Pamplona and the bulls. I am Corpus Christi
and birds on powerlines—stitches on a grey face.

The sky swells like a bruise over me, and my feet
cannot stop kicking at concrete that refuses to laugh.

Falling into time with my heart, I kick to keep warm.
I am being judged by black, feathered fists.

One by one, fears and secrets smoke from my lips,
breath hovers and fades, fails to shadow my face.

I am hiding my hands and hoping for stillness.
I am pacing in my blood – the birds want me to run.

It is every morning, 6am, and they shit and laugh
their machine gun chat, cuts of sound swarming.

I am only the archive of this dawn. When I cough,
birds scatter from the wires like buckshot.

Coconut

I hurled one to the sky and hoped,
let it drop and hit the sidewalk.
Did it again. Did it until
it split, a cloud stream
trickling from coarse brown skin.

This, when young, and my tía yelled:
Enséñame que macho eres—
and ran me out with the rough, hairy
rock. I knew I couldn't return
until I wrecked a way inside.

Brown faces hurled hard words at me:
coconut rolled into *pocho* which cracked
into *¿Quién crees que eres?* something
I keep asking myself, tasking myself
to answer, and certain I can't.

Mandilón followed my first marriage,
whispered by a couple watching me
wade through bras with my then-wife,
a white woman who said I should *Man up*
when I translated this new label to her.

¿quién soy? I am the quiet tears
trickling down my coarse brown skin.
I am a wrecked güey—way, way inside.
I am a question asking itself, my self
whispered by those watching me.

Disrepair

I turn to another blank page and write:
The rain falls from the sky in disrepair.

Oregon: walks through fog into more fog.
Does the heart, like mist, repair?

In pentimenti, you glimpse what came before;
the past, what brushstrokes can't repair.

In the divorce, I gave up half my books;
my inner shelves were left in disrepair.

We discuss our exes now in calmer voices.
At first, we cried, whispered, hissed repair.

Scanning again the Seven Deadly Sins,
my devil heart feels they list Repair.

I've had to go for love like Sappho's scraps.
I've cracked, been lost; dismissed repair.

The rain falls from the sky in disrepair—
I write, as if the words promised repair.

Arguing for the Stars

for ani

In the Egyptian Book of the Dead
there are those who believed the night sky
to be an iron plate, stars torches
   hung over the world,

and those who believed the night to be
a goddess adorned in stars. Between
torches and jewelry believers
   argued, side by side,

their voices dying down as the dark
grew, leaving only silence and those
points of light above them holding still.
   There are nights you point

out a star, and without looking I
say it is a plane, a satellite,
something other than what you say. Such
   is my disbelief,

not in stars, but in being able
to see anything clearly from here.
You argue for your stars, and your words
   help me. The night sky

   fills again with what
   you would have me see.

Conditioning (Air Study)

Conditioning is what is done with
soldiers, the heads of children
and dogs, what is studied

in the swipe and tap of
our fingers across screens.
Conditioning is

your legs red at noon,
the concrete of a city blurred
by the same fever

falling in sheets
of sweat down your back,
your head ringing,

swimming in light. Conditioning is
the hubris of weather by button,
the shift-of-belt-buckle mentality of:

It don't matter even
the holes in the sky
or the waste in the water,

we can fix this, fight
the sun's mad knuckle.

*

Your tía hates it when you block the fan
while she watches TV. Any time you do,
a sandal shoots past your head

and smacks the glass
like a fish flopped on concrete,
that sad sound of being

out of place. You are used to it.
Used to sunflower seed shells
popped between teeth

counting down each salty
second. Used to the shells
collecting in the trash

like the black and white
wings of some creature
that has to be gnashed at

for the summer to pass.

*

Walking down the hall
and feeling the cold
seep through the cracks

of other people's places
activates thoughts
of faces working outside

when the sun scolds
skin raw, forgets
how to hold back;

thoughts of another life
where you walked down streets
until your shoelaces

were bit away
to the knot,
and nights

where you held a small
fold of dollars
like aces

allowing you to sit
a little longer, hold
a coffee in a diner

a little longer
when it got too bad
outside; thoughts of

how it's always bad
even when it's not
your hand anymore

or your back
just your impoverished
pride walking beside you,

feeling the cold
like a voice rising
in another room

shutting you down
to a whisper in the margins
of someone else's argument.

*

Down the aisle of a bus
with a broken A/C,
a boy follows his mother,

his whole body shoved forward
by the clamber
and shuck

of a stop.
His open palm
hits his mother's waist;

she swats it,
switches
her cell phone

to the ear closest
to him. Without looking up,
the boy tries again,

his fingers,
in the air he'd have hold him,
spread,

let through light.

On the Times I Don't Remember the Right Words for Things

Tonight, leaving work after a double shift,
    what is left to say on my walk home,
in and out of conversation with myself,

dims and leaves me surprised: *hone o oru,*
    a phrase I read, I couldn't say when,
comes back clearly, scratched across a book's flyleaf

with the words it might translate to in English
    (*to break your bones,* or *to have a bone
broken*) in pencil scrawled and smudged beside it,

as if whoever tried to work it out stopped,
    unable to choose between doing
the breaking and being broken, and left both

phrases for me like answers to a riddle
    no one is around to ask, and which
I no longer have the breath to decipher,

unable to read the growing night against
    the headlights of oncoming traffic,
each pair of lights indifferent, reading past me—

another breath slips, breaks my conversation,
    words again have a falling-leaves feel:
the feel of a foot driven into the air

of a missing step, that braced stagger, the feel
   of reaching for a door you thought closed
only to find it open, your artless hand

on the air you have to walk through to move on.

Saudade

after the painting by José Ferraz de Almeida Júnior

My wife catches me with the painting
on my computer screen and I say,
It's Saudade, as if the woman engrossed
in her letter, leaning against the open
window were named after this feeling of
longing for something absent, a place or
person one loves.

I set Saudade as the wallpaper on
my computer, and whenever I write in
my journal—poetry, daily life, tarot cards—
I close everything so that Saudade alone
is there, busy with her words, clutching
her black shawl to her mouth, each
          breath caught there.

This is how we stand with cellphones—
I say this one afternoon, without warning,
without a conversation between us, without even
meaning to. I retrace my thinking while
my wife remembers the painting with me:
woman reading in another life, a portrait
      of being without.

Is this the face I made when
I stood reading my wife's text telling
about eight people being shot in our
neighborhood within 24 hours as I waited
to board a plane back to her,
believing and not believing, the words pulsing
         with each breath?

Is this the face she made waiting
for me to call while at Canto
right after the mass shooting a week
earlier, Pulse in the air as a poet
sang: *Pulso! Pulso! Pulso!* until the room
I sat in pulsed with attention, with
              presence and life?

Is this the face my friend made
as he sat in the same audience,
the poet's words taking him elsewhere, other
faces, he told me later it meant
the world to have an elder poet
speak to the younger generation, meaning we
        spoke of listening?

Is this the face I would see
reflected between photos and clips of Aleppo,
scenes of rubble and ruins that push
me back into myself, until there is
no self just silence, a finger swiping
a screen, and eyes that cannot see
           clearly fast enough?

Saudade, I am dark-haired like you, as
tied to words and silence as you;
as I go gray do I grow
less or more like you? The more
I write, the more I am left
to rewrite; Saudade, words change the more
          we read them.

The photo of the poet Zurita standing
in the water one must walk through
to read "The Sea of Pain" has
him looking elsewhere. Saudade, his work is
an installation, a work of presence. Instead
of just liking it, I should be
        doing something too.

Googling Saudade, I find a video where
one man says you can't translate it,
another that you can't touch it. Saudade,
in your painting your eyes are half-closed,
the words near memorized, the paper, presence
only. You leave me the distance implied
       in a word.

From a professor: *You're looking at survival,*
where there aren't standards. You want wisdom,
but accept sonority as substitute. You might
find an editor, a readership; you might
not. A white ear schooled in white
lit. will consider this torqued towards melodrama.
　　　　Unique, not enough.

Questions After the Election

In her story

about being told

by her white bosses'

white secretaries

Vote Trump! You

better vote Trump!

as she punched out

from work

as usual, tired

and body-sore,

does my mother know

she gathered

the darkness of each

corner of the factory,

and the darkness

of the drive home

switching between stations,

nothing sounding right,

and the darkness

in her mind

listing

all the work

waiting

for her at home,

and the darkness of

the night over

Corpus Christi,

and how these

darknesses spill over now

into every word

I'm urged to write,

because nights like these

are ink, and her story

of pretending not to hear,

but telling me

what she heard,

what was said,

is a story of darknesses

being separated, made distinct

as words on a page,

which hold darkness

in one form until

we close our eyes

and darkness shifts

to darkness

shifted—

at the end

of her shift,

does she know

about the darkness

I will hold

for her?

Notes, Credits, Acknowledgments

American Studies: The italicized lines in the last section of this poem are from a poem by Faiz Ahmad Faiz, translated and quoted mid-conversation by friend and poet, Adeeba Shahid Talukder. A variation of Talukder's translation of these lines can also be found cited in *The Adroit Journal* interview, "To the Limits of Sight: A Conversation with Adeeba Shahid Talukder": https://theadroitjournal.org/2019/08/20/to-the-limits-of-sight-a-conversation-with-adeeba-shahid-talukder/.

*

Credit: Juan Felipe Herrera, excerpts from "Mexican Differences Mexican Similarities" from *187 Reasons Mexicans Can't Cross the Border: Undocuments 1971-2007.* Copyright © 2007 by Juan Felipe Herrera. Reprinted with the permission of The Permissions Company, LLC, on behalf of City Lights, www.citylights.com.

Credit: Excerpt from "The Dry Salvages" from FOUR QUARTETS by T.S. Eliot. Copyright © 1941 by T.S. Eliot, renewed 1969 by Esme Valerie Eliot. Reprinted by permission of Mariner Books, an imprint of HarperCollins Publishers. All rights reserved.

Credit: Christopher Morley, excerpt from "The Watchman's Sonnet." Reprinted by permission of Christopher Morley Literary Estate.

Credit: Excerpts from "Acquainted with the Night" by Robert Frost, public domain.

Credit: From "I Sleep A Lot", from The Collected Poems: 1931-1987 by Czeslaw Milosz. Copyright (c) 1988 by Czeslaw Milosz Royalties, Inc. Used by permission of HarperCollins Publishers.

*

Publication Acknowledgements

Special thanks to the editors and staff of the following publications where poems from this collection have been previously published, at times in previous versions:

A Dozen Nothing: "En la colonia I cannot find," "Night Matter,"
     "Conditioning (Air Study)," "Questions After the Election"
Boog City: "Birthday Dirge"
Borderlands: Texas Poetry Review: "Language Dirge"
Crab Orchard Review: "Selena: a study of reoccurrence / worry"
Hunger Mountain: "Conditioning (Run Study)"
Kansas City Voices: "Arguing for the Stars"
North American Review: "Saudade"
Pilgrimage: "Coconut"
Prairie Schooner: "Race," "Disrepair"
Profane Journal: "In the margins, with blackberries"
Qu Literary Magazine: "Engrossed"
Stirring: "In the margins, with birds"
Sugar House Review: "On the Times I Don't Remember the Right
     Words for Things"
Terrain.org: "American Studies"

"Snow in December" and "October, before the Election" were originally published in *Turn: an anthology* (Uttered Chaos, 2013).

"A Poco" was published as part of the essay "Keeping the Conversation Going, or Some Stories I Can't Tell Without Rolling My R's: A Meditation on Latinidad, Disidentification, & Some Poems" in *Far Villages: Welcome Essays for New and Beginner Poets*. Ed. Abayomi Animashaun (Black Lawrence Press, 2020).

Photo: Ani Schreiber

José Angel Araguz, Ph.D. is the author of *Rotura* (Black Lawrence Press, 2022). His poetry and prose have appeared in *Prairie Schooner, Poetry International, The Acentos Review,* and *Oxidant | Engine* among other places. He is an Assistant Professor at Suffolk University where he serves as Editor-in-Chief of *Salamander* and is also a faculty member of the Solstice Low-Residency MFA Program. He blogs and reviews books at *The Friday Influence.*